LOVE ON THE ROCKS

By Marianne LaValle-Vincent

DEDICATION

This book is dedicated to all who have loved and lost. And to those lucky enough to still be smack dab in the middle of happily ever after. I applaud you.

And—

To my daughter, Jess who has kissed enough toads, fools and paupers! I wish for her the love of a good man with the heart of a warrior, the patience of a saint and the wallet of a billionaire!

Love on the rocks

Ain't no surprise

Just pour me a drink and I'll tell you some lies

Got nothin' to lose so you just sing the blues

All the time

Neil Diamond

Contents

THE WINTER OF MY DISCONTENT

winter soothes me so
as if the frost could preserve
my very existence
and keep me safe from
what I fear
like a shield
the snow surrounds me
and guards my forever
frozen heart
so none can
penetrate
or sting

and the barren trees
remind me
there is still time
for hibernation
before the inevitable
thaw
melts my heart
again
and I will
hurt
    and feel
  and taste
what you took
away
when it was warm

I watch as the snow
falls into a blanket of
sparkle
and remember when
it used to shine
for me

***Winter is much like unrequited love—cold and merciless
Kellie Elmore

BLINDSIGHTED

never saw it
coming
I only felt the
sting
and the emptiness
of your
departure
leaving me to
once again
take the
blame
and the
responsibility
of your
failures

never expected the
loneliness
or the
ache
from your
disappearance
trapping me in
solitude
to focus on my
faults
and my naivety'

I expected too
much
from you
for you could give
nothing
but disappointment
and even that
was better
than this

*****Blinded by the light——*

SURVIVAL OF THE FITTEST

the same song plays
over and over
again
like a sword
it penetrates my
soul
bringing you here
for a while
again

wrapping my arms around
your memory
I fill myself with
you
humming those notes
that played for
us
like a private
symphony

how did I survive
> *how did I breathe*
without your existence
how did I pick myself up
knowing
> finally understanding
the depth of your
demise

people call me a survivor
but I am just going through the
motions
of life after your
death

Life asked death: Why do people love me but hate you?

And death responded: Because you are a beautiful lie and I am a
painful truth

YOU SAID YOU WOULD, YOU LIAR

you promised our love
would be like no other
before us
and no one
after
you swore eternity
would end
before
we would part
you whispered forever
and a day
and my heart
believed
    I believed
you swallowed me
whole
like an ocean
and left nothing
but the waves of
misery
that wash continually
over me

you *lied*
for you felt nothing
    nothing but
comfort for just a short
time
and I made it easy for you to

leave
but I lied, too
because I am not
ok
without you

*****Tell me lies tell me sweet little lies*

THE MONSTER UNDERNEATH

I wonder if it will surface
tonight
like so many nights
before
if it will come out of
hiding
to strip me of
my significance
and take away
that last ounce of
dignity
it rears its ugly
head
after you've thrown back a
few
and spews forth
the ugliness I've learned
to expect
from all your vicious
truths
that only you can rationalize
that *monster* who sometimes
hides
sometimes stays hidden
for an eternity
or so it seems
always returns when you feed
your addiction
it doesn't take much

to bring him around
just a swallow or
three
for that ugly beast to
rip me to the
bone
while you sleep
and dream of
my perfection

"Here's to alcohol—the rose-colored glasses of life"
                                        F. Scott Fitzgerald

FAREWELL TO YOUTH

infallible at 18
I ruled the
world
chose the path
less traveled
but only went half
way
scoffed at sadness
until it invaded
my person
and dared to mock
death
until I felt its cold hand
I laughed at loneliness
yet it captured me
and I shunned those
in pain
until I ached from
my ego
hasn't it been hundreds of
years
since my youth
since the freedom of my
innocence paved the
way
or did I just let it slip
into oblivion
with the other treasures
I neglected to savor

goodbye, my youth
like an ember
you burned out too
soon
and I reach, now with my aged
hand to hold on
for just a little longer

"Youth is easily deceived because it is quick to hope"
Aristotle

FAULTS

I am not your
fault
my own creation
brought me to this
point
the sins are
mine
the lies I gave birth
to
died only because I
buried them

I am not the result
of your
disappearance
you did not define
me
nor did you
destroy who I
am
I did that alone
with help from
no one

you did not
break me
or rip my soul
from my wounded chest
or place these scars

on my being
I would never give you
that much credit
you only made me
stronger
because you still believe
it was never your
fault

***The snag about marriage is it's not worth the divorce

RAIN

I used to believe that the
rain
would wash away the
hurt
that this holy water of sorts
could cure
almost anything
how brave of me
to never use an
umbrella
or take shelter from
the storm
how heroic I was
to allow myself to be
drenched
like a fool
praying for a
miracle

how can this falling deluge
drown the
soul
and wash away the
good along with the
bad
and sometimes bring
sadness along with
the darkness that we try so
hard to avoid

it's only a lucky few
that ever find the rainbow
after the storm
but for me the rain is just another way
to wash away what was

"I love walking in the rain cause no one can see me crying"

Charlie Chaplin

THE GARDEN

she plants in dirt full of
weeds
and up come
roses
I place seeds of perfect flowers
in perfectly tended soil
and up come
weeds
she barely works at the
garden
and it smiles
and is evergreen
and I water and feed
and tend it ever so carefully
yet it
dies
again and again

I work at loving
you
as if it were my
job
and she doesn't even
try
yet she has your
heart and
she claims the fruits of your
garden
while I am busy pulling

the weeds
she will have room to
grow
and you will stop to smell
her roses
and never even notice
our garden never blooms
anymore

****I created a garden of Eden, and all you did was offer me
an apple"*

Marianne LaValle-Vincent

I DIDN'T LIKE HIM WHEN I LIKED HIM

he was always just a
diversion
just a rebound
after the devastation
he found me almost
irresistible
and it was exactly what I
needed
he made me laugh
and loved me from his bones
I was his drug
injecting myself into his very
being
I knew it was a temporary
fix
but I didn't care
        I didn't hurt for him
I still hurt for me
        for my addiction
and I used his affection
like a narcotic
hoping it would take away the pain
and the memories
but it never worked
like we never worked
my addiction
remains
and cuts to my
soul

I threw him away
because I was over it
yet I hope he's still
hooked
because misery *loves*
company
and because without
misery
I'd probably be over
you

"I don't think misery loves any damn thing at all"

Bruce Machart

VINCENT

at a little
nite café
I fell in love with
you
surrounded by the
sunflowers
and the
mulberry trees
we were merely
a pair of lovers
inhaling the
starry nite
when you took me
in the
poppy field
amongst the
thatched cottages
and I inhaled the hypnotic
fragrance of the
irises
as I watched you
young man with a hat
walking on the
bridge in the rain
yet forever remaining
a vision
in the *Orchard*

And when no hope was left in site
On that starry, starry nite, you took your life as lovers often do—
   but I could have told you, Vincent—this world was
never meant
   for one as beautiful as you

WHY I'M SOMETIMES A BITCH

when people think it's funny
cause I really hate to camp
but yet they still try to change my mind
they really should revamp

I'm not at home in the great outdoors
so not a nature lover
a picnic is for ants and bugs
from that I'd never recover

not into polyester
or elastic waisted slacks
don't try to tell me to act my age
I may have an anxiety attack

I get annoyed if you're walking too slow
or if you're bad at math
don't use improper English
it puts me on the warpath

I hate when men think they can grocery shop
please just stay the hell at home
cause you'll only end up calling the wife
from your attached at the hip Iphone

if I invite you to dinner
don't come without some wine
I refuse to dine without the grape
it's part of my Italian bloodline

so yes, I'm can be bitchy
and sometimes full of gloom
just be sure there's always a space
for me to park my broom

tread lightly when you're with me
try not to change my mood
just avoid my every single pet peeve
or literally——you're screwed!

"Bitch, please!! You've got more issues than Vogue"

WHEN I STILL BELIEVED IN LOVE

every Friday evening
he would bring me
pink roses
and baby's breath
and I would place them
in my most radiant
vase
and they lived there
beautiful and
alive
reminding me throughout the week
of the love he
vowed
they were perfect
just like us
and then one Friday
there were no more
roses
the vase was empty
and devoid of
life
outside it was bleak
like something had
died
but it was months
before I realized
it was us
I thought those roses
would bloom

forever
but like love sometimes
does
they faded
and died
leaving me with barely enough
breath to inhale
the aroma of
yesterday

***Who wants flowers when they're dead—nobody!
      J.D. Salinger—The Catcher in the Rye

WATCHING FROM THE SIDELINES

I watched as he
broke her
leaving her in so many
pieces
it was impossible to
repair
her shattered heart
exposed and bloody
for all to see
and I couldn't mend
her
I couldn't make it
better
and I ached from her
pain
and withered from her
broken soul

eyes that looked to me for
comfort
and relief
that begged for remission
tore me to the
quick
yet I could not fight
this mutation of
love
nor could I offer her
a cure

her wounds will heal
and her heart will somehow
fuse together
but I will never be whole
again
she will someday forgive
but I will hate him
even after
death

Love needs too much help—hate takes care of itself

A PERFECT FOOL

perfection escapes most
mortals
it's usually found in something
that doesn't breathe
or feel
     or bleed
I have held the perfect
rose
and inhaled the perfection of
the stars and the moon
yet once upon a time
I thought I'd found
it
the perfect love
love that nurtures
and grows
love that knows only
the afterglow of
passion
and the foreplay
of a promise

and I remember when you left
you lied and said I was the nearest thing
to perfection you had ever known
but you neglected to tell me
I was only
a perfect fool
for I actually believed you were just

foolish enough to love
only me

Ah, what fools these mortals be!
William Shakespeare

IN YOUR DREAMS, BABY!

am I your fantasy
I asked
and just as I knew you would
you lied
and told me
yes
and am I everything you will ever
want
and again you lied
and said
of course
and you whispered to me
as only lovers do
that you would love me
forever and a
day
for I was a dream come
true
the answer to your
prayers
the best thing since sliced
bread

and I asked if we were meant to
be
and oh—how I wanted you to lie
but you said you loved me too
much
to lead me on

and you walked away
leaving me with only the
fantasy
you created

> ****I have too many fantasies to be a house-
> wife—I guess I'll be someone's fantasy

Marilyn Monroe

I'VE GOT THE WORLD ON A STRING

I never expected to be a
marionette
someone's little puppet
in my wildest dreams
I never thought you could
control my every
thought
my every
emotion
you pull the string
and I dance with complete
abandonment
a tiny dancer
for you to
dominate
a pawn for you to
manipulate

and you play me
like a fine tuned
violin
again and again
you call for an
encore
as I give you the performance
of a lifetime

I ask only for a small bit of
applause

every once in a while
before these strings are
severed
and the final curtain
falls

    I've got the world on a string—sitting on a
rainbow. Got the string around my
     finger—what a world, what a life——I'm in love!
           Frank Sinatra

HURTS SO GOOD

how amusing that we both loved the same
person
that your narcissistic
pleasures
were satiated by only
you
incapable of feeling love
you exist for your own
entertainment

your sadistic side
actually turned out to be
your best
side
for even the hurt
felt good
even the pain you inflicted
was a small sign of
humanity
something for me to
cling to
other than the
whipping post

and my prayers are different
now
now that I am free from your
prison
my only wish is for you to drown

in your own
reflection
and drink from your own cup of
poison
and I hope it hurts
like love

Come on baby make it hurt so good!

CRIMINAL MINDS

ah—the ideas that have crossed my
mind
frightening even those with the strongest
will
plotting and planning
the crime of the century
thinking only of the sweet taste of
victory
deciding on my weapon of
choice
poison
        hand gun
                knife
or maybe just a repeat
performance
of your abomination
how were you not
convicted?
you destroyed me
        annihilated me
murdered my soul
and you walked
away
you actually got away
with it
and I am the one
doing hard time
I only dream of revenge
hurting you to the core

      bringing you to your
knees
but it will never happen
you would have to *feel something*
you need to *have a heart* for me to
break
and we both know
you are but an empty shell
that will never, ever
shatter

      ***Funny thing about revenge—it can make a
killer out of a nun*

Kevis Hendrickson

BETTE DAVIS EYES

you said I had eyes like
her
but you didn't know her
not like I did
you didn't know how she
died in *Dark Victory*
or that she was a killer in
What Ever happened to Baby Jane
you never understood her
soul
or how she felt when she was
The Bad Sister
so how would you recognize
her eyes
how could you know that my eyes
were like hers
when you never knew
me
tears that filled brown eyes like an
ocean of pain
were never her
eyes
they were mine
but you wanted me to play a
minor part
in your play about
love
while you were the
star

but if you really, *really* knew
Bette
you'd know she never played *anything*
but the lead

      ****She's precocious and she knows just what it*
takes to make a pro blush
        She's got Greta Garbo stand-off sighs
          She's got Bette Davis Eyes
               Kim Karnes

A THORN BETWEEN THE ROSES

for the longest time
I only saw the roses
inhaling their aroma
and their beauty
it mattered not
their color
it was the symbolism
I loved
and when I touched them
it was as if velvet
caressed my fingertips
soft and inviting
and the buds were like
constant promises
and then I felt the
sting
and bled from the
puncture
yet I never knew
the rose could
bite
I never saw the
thorn
it was as if it were never
there
for all I ever saw
was the perfection of its
bloom

I look for the thorns
now
and I'm sometimes astonished
by its floret
yet I am still unprepared
for the sting
from that ever deceptive
rose

"A rose by any other name would smell as sweet"
William Shakespeare

LOOKS LIKE WE MADE IT

I saw you yesterday
arm in arm with
her
and you were laughing
and holding her hand
it made me cling a little
tighter
to him
bringing him closer to
me
as if I were afraid
to let him
go
and a flood of
memories
poured over me
forcing those scars to open
and bleed
like it was a moment
ago
when we were
that couple
surrounded by the promise
of forever
and I wonder if you are telling her
the very same
lies
and if you ever
wonder

if I'm telling them
too
I guess I'm ok
with him
like you probably are
with her
but isn't it sad that we
didn't make it work
for us

*****I am more than just my scars*
Andrew Davidson

LOVE ON THE ROCKS

it's 3 am when I roll
over
instinctively reaching
for you
but you're not
there
your side of the bed is
cold
like it usually is
on Tuesdays and
Fridays
for those are your days with
her
you think I still don't
know
but I've known
forever
you told me with your
kiss
and the way you don't look
at me
anymore

our bed is cold
on those empty
nights
but it's even colder
on the nights you're
home

it's just so *God damn hard*
to sleep
with *her*
in the middle
because there's just never enough room
for all that horrible
deception

       She will never be welcome for she is your trans-
gression——not mine

MASTERPIECE

I took those broken
pieces
and tried to put them back
together
but they remained
jagged and
torn
I couldn't make them fit
not like they used
to
something was
missing
and nothing filled the
holes that were left by the
break

I finally threw those broken pieces
away
and began to create something
new
and it took a while
but it came together
like a masterpiece
the colors are even
brighter and
I think it's my best
work
so far

cause I've dropped it a few
times
and it never, ever
breaks

***Art is to console those who are broken by life
                                        Vincent Van Gogh

CLOUDY DAYS

I don't need to
pretend
on cloudy days
don't need to fake
that sunny disposition
loosing myself in the
gray gloom
somehow makes me feel
as if I blend in
like one of the rain
drops
and there's comfort in those dismal
clouds
I know just what to
expect
the inevitable rain
and the deluge of
fog
hides me from the
reality
that will soon
follow

some say they wait for the clouds
to lift
for the proverbial storm to
pass
but I've been stronger than the
storm

since I can't remember
when
and I am more than at home
in this *cyclone*
you call life

"The air up there in the clouds is very pure and fine, bracing and
delicious. And why shouldn't it be? —it is the same the angels
breathe."

Mark Twain

DEATH BY LOVE

I don't remember
coming back to
life
only being able to
breathe again
not a deep breath
but a small gasp
for the pain was
unbearable
time was forever
gone
and it seemed as if
there were no more
colors
in the world
there was no time
anymore
it just stood still
minutes faded into
hours
and it was always
so dark
for nothing could
penetrate
my mutilated
heart
I thought only of
what might have been
and how much you must have

hurt
but your death killed me, too
that fatal gunshot
you inflicted
got us both
but you're the only one
who doesn't feel the pain
anymore

When people kill themselves, they think they're ending the pain,
but all they're doing is
                    passing it on to those they leave behind."
                                        Jeanette Walls

ONCE UPON A MIDNIGHT DREARY

God, I used to love
midnight
have you any idea how beautiful
the stars and the moon
shone?
the sky became a
pallet
for each evening's
creation
and I would loose
myself in the atmosphere of
the heavens
as if I were the only human
able to capture its
symmetry
and if I looked long enough
and hard enough
I could see your light
shinning just for me
that one perfect
star
that I always knew
was you
but your star has somehow
faded
or maybe it's just my
perception of the
sky
after all these years
the moon and the stars

just don't hang the same
way for me
since you left
and midnight is just a time
to say *goodbye*

    Once upon a midnight dreary, while I pondered weak
and weary—

Edgar Allen Poe

IT'S A QUARTER TO THREE

the bar is full of people
with nowhere else to go
cause who the hell would want
this pack of
losers
the vodka goes down
easily
promises start to fly
and out come the lies
Jesus— no one wants to
spend the night
alone
the plaid shirt leans in towards me
and asks if I've got a cigarette
I tell him he shouldn't smoke
cause he's got enough problems
with his alcohol abuse
he's obviously not at all amused
so I ask him what he's really
looking for
and he tells me
he wants a good time
just a friend to spend the night with
after I tell him he can't afford me
and I'll never be his friend
he gets up and walks away
and shoots me an evil stare
and I really don't give a damn
cause what I'm looking for sure as hell

isn't him
but it just might be at the bottom of
my next glass of *Grey Goose*
it just depends on
my mood
and who's buying
cause even a queen can be bought
if the time and price is right

"One more drink, and I'll be under the host"
      Mae West

BLACK MAGIC

under your spell
mesmerized
by the feeling
I wish only for
a continuance
of your witchcraft
hypnotic though you
are
I am unafraid
as you lure me to your
coven
blinded by the lies
that promise nothing but
an eternal abyss
demonic eyes
and a soul of black
are your offerings
yet I accept
for there is no other
choice
but to follow you
as you take me deeper and
deeper
into your hell
and I surrender
as you knew I
would
preparing myself for the
fire

that will scar
like so many times
before
but between heaven and
hell
there is only a void
and I would rather burn
with you
than fly with the angels

****You can't argue with Satan—for he is the greatest
debater of all time*

Billy Graham

CLOTHES MAKE THE MAN

I'm a sucker for a man
in a tux
looking so perfect
and formal
in that rigid bow tie
that just about
chokes him
makes me want to
rip it off
and set him free
gotta love a guy
in jeans and
maybe a polo
by *Ralph Lauren*
in a manly shade of
blue
he's just relaxed as
hell
and ready for anything
but I think my favorite
might be the trench coat
belted and protective
cause you just never know
what you'll find
underneath
and just for the
record
I prefer boxers
to briefs

because once we get to your
birthday suit
brief is not what I want
cause I can sing
happy birthday
all night long

     Girls do not dress for men—they dress for themselves and other women.

     If they dressed for men, they'd walk around naked all the time

Betsey Johnson

STAGES OF LOVE

(stage one, beginnings)

you meet
and there's an instant
attraction
perhaps over dinner
you'll exchange some
trivialities
when in reality
you're both thinking about
when you'll sleep together
so polite and sweet
complimenting each other's
looks
and clothing
        and intellect
and it doesn't mean shit
cause you're not real
not yet
it's all just a mask
it's all just a lure
the little white lies
and the pretense
of innocence

that first kiss
so magical
offering all those promises
of tomorrow

and the burning desire to enter
stage two

> *You're the only one who can survive your story,*
the only one who
>> can write your future

Tessa Shaffer

SHE'S GOT LEGS

perhaps you should speak
a bit more quietly
into your cell
when you're speaking
of her
her and her friggin
legs
legs that go on
forever
a body to die for
God—how did you get
so lucky?
the envy of all your
friends
23 years old and all she wants
is you
and you give no thought
to me
and my short little
legs
legs that used to be
enough
a body that carried your
children
I have to give her
credit
she's a fox, all right!
she saw that bulge
in your pocket

your wallet you fool
and she's gonna use
those legs
to walk all over
you
and I will use these
unwanted legs
to simply
walk away

She's got legs—she knows how to use them
ZZ Top

HOW TO HAVE SEX WITHOUT REALLY TRYING

maybe he offers you a shoulder
to cry on
or you watch a movie together
maybe you had a bad day at work
and he offers you a massage
I mean you're friends, right
what's the harm
a couple glasses of
wine
maybe you cook a simple
supper
he just wants to thank you
so he gives you a little kiss
no biggie
and you make that fatal mistake:
you kiss him back
so it's morning
and it's awkward as hell
cause last night was nice
but you want him to leave
or——
you plan on telling him it really
didn't mean anything
but he's gone when you awaken
and either way it sucks
it just never should have happened
fast forward a few weeks
and you're lonely as hell

so you shoot him a text
and the next thing you know
it's happening again
but it's just sex
nothing more nothing less
and remember this:
every single woman alive
has to have a backup plan
and sex is no big deal
until you aren't getting any!

Sex is the consolation you have when you can't have love
Gabriel Garcia Marquez

STAGES OF LOVE

(stage 2—in the thick of it)

it's all passion and
sex
those butterflies in the
stomach
sweaty palms and
heart palpitations
dressing to
kill
everything and anything
for him
each and every waking moment
he consumes your every
thought
life is almost
perfect
the colors of the world are
brighter
every love song plays
for you
and there's an undeniable
hope for the
future
you check your phone
every two seconds for a
text
and even work is a happier
place
it's love

you foolish little girl
hit by the thunderbolt
you are disappearing
into him
welcome to the best part
enjoy it while it lasts
and have no fear of perfection
for you will never, ever
reach it

True love will never die. Even if it ends and you find another—
It will haunt you for the rest of your life

JUST A BRIEF AFFAIR

it was no big deal
just a brief little
indiscretion
a few evenings at a sordid
motel
maybe a bite to eat
before the festivities
no bullshit
        no promises
just a roll in the hay
an uninhibited frolic
almost like an unwritten
agreement
we won't get attached
and God knows I didn't
want to
but I did
Jesus Christ *I did*
and I lived for those
nights
when you held me in your
arms
it was euphoric
and in my heart I wanted to believe
you felt the same way
but you never did
not even for a minute

in the end
it was me that broke it
off
I walked away
because
you never would have
and I envy you
your detachment
and your nonchalance
and I wish I could have
settled
for second best

****You broke me the hardest*

WHO THE HELL ARE BARNUM & BAILEY

I hate the friggin
circus
what the hell's to like?
am I supposed to get excited
about elephants and
trapeze artists
and don't even get me started
about the clowns
and what about all that
dirt?
Christ—it's almost as bad as the zoo
or going on a friggin picnic
can you understand why we
never made it
you loved all that shit
I knew it would never last
when you dragged me to the
state fair
I was in the midway
literally fighting for my life
and you were never more at ease
and those buildings
filled with cows and chickens
and shit
I can't
a million years ago
you took me to see *Barbra Streisand*
in central park

and I was beyond happy
but you must have misunderstood me
and who I was
because that was the *only time*
I tolerated the outdoors
and the dirt *and you*
and I thought you knew
I'm an indoor kinda gal
and I'd never end up with *anyone*
whose idea of fun is a circus

****Never go to sleep with a clown in your room*

WHAT'S LOVE GOT TO DO WITH IT

it's just a knee jerk
reaction
just a little spark of
electricity
nothing major
maybe a momentary glance
that lasts more than a moment
or the touch of his hand
purely by accident
a flirtatious little touch
or a little teasing smile
is just a little bit of nothing
it's not a big deal
so you have a couple drinks
and maybe a dance or two
a kiss is just a kiss
it's anything but
love
call it passion
or enthusiasm
call it purely physical
an animal attraction
or lust
but never think it's
love
because love is pain
it's a beautiful ache but it's still
pain
and trust me

you're much better off lusting
cause when the smoke clears
sex is just sex baby
and you can walk away
but if you're in love
it changes everything
and even if you do walk away
it will follow you forever

                        ***What's love but a second-hand emotion?*
                                                Tina Turner

IT'S JUST A BROKEN HEART

I mean no one ever died from a
broken heart——right?
the tears won't stop and the
pain is excruciating
but it's nothing serious
you can hardly get out of
bed
or talk or walk
but it's not like you're sick
or hurt
    or damaged goods
and your friends are telling you
to get over it
move on
    get a life
but you're too hung up on the
old one to even take a step
in another direction
and there's that ever-present ache
in your gut
that feels like you've been
stabbed
about a hundred million times
you can't eat or sleep
you're a hot mess
but what's the big deal
it's not like you're dying
it just feels that way
and for the first time *ever*

you have no confidence
no self-worth
not even a drop of happiness
can be found in your entire body
but it's nothing, really
so your heart's been ripped in pieces
what's the big deal
you didn't really ever want to breathe
again—did you?

****You must have thought I was bullet proof*

STARDUST

the sand from the stars
filled my eyes
the night we met
and I remember your silhouette
lit by the bright
crescent moon
the navy-blue sky
intoxicating and plush
shone like a silver
brilliance
a million stars
shooting up above us
sent signals of
passion and devotion
the scene was perfect
for me to love you
and I did
like a moth to a flame
you drew me in

how could I know that the stars
would fade
or that some evenings there is no
moon
no silver lining or promise of
forever
and even the sky looks chalky and
pale
when you're just trying to survive

it's funny how you can miss something
you never really had——
I should have captured the moon
when I had the chance
and it sure would be nice to have a
star to guide me
cause I really am afraid
of the dark

    ***And now my consolation is in the stardust of a song

Hoagy Carmichael

THANKS FOR THE MAMMORIES

the first things that anyone saw
were my boobs though I thought them a flaw
I was just too darn short
and my clothes they'd distort
for those pendulous bouncing eye draws

now most men would argue the fact
that it's sexy as hell to be stacked
but the truth of the matter
is they just make you fatter
and from your intellect they'll always subtract

so I said to the girls "listen up"
I'm tired of overflowing these cups
so a surgeon we'll find
with a beyond brilliant mind
who will help me get rid of these pups

under the knife I did go
and it sure did cost me some dough
but it was worth every cent
for the doc to reinvent
those beautiful C cup combos

now the girls are a perky little pair
they're just friggin perfect, I swear
I've never been chaste

more than a handful's a waste
and I'm happy as hell, I declare!!!

*****Boobs—proof that men can focus on two
things at once*

SHATTERED

afraid to stand
for fear I'll
crumble
I remain in the
fetal position
afraid of the light
the pain washes over me
like a flood
and I'm drowning in the
loss
gasping for air
I don't want to
remember
but I am inundated with the
deluge of yesterday
yesterday that seems like an
eternity before
yesterday when I was alive
unscathed by love
        able to inhale
the blissful aroma of tomorrow
I am suddenly made of
glass
see through and
vulnerable
and it is just a matter of
time

before I am completely
shattered

*Such heaps of broken glass to sweep away—you'd think
the inner dome of heaven had fallen*

Robert Frost

JUST ONE OF THOSE THINGS

it was just one time
just one little indiscretion
it meant nothing
it was just sex
there were no feelings involved
I thought of you the whole time
it was different
I was drunk
so was she
what's the big deal
it meant nothing
it'll never happen again
I told you I was drunk
I never meant to hurt you
you're overreacting
can't we just forget it ever happened
I'm not gonna tell you her name
she means nothing to me
why are you packing?
what are you doing?
let me explain
please don't go
it was just the one time
no, I am not in love with her
you're still packing
ok—it was more than once
she means nothing to me
she's not you
I love you

I'm sorry
goodbye world

> ***You went and broke us. You are so much worse than a cheater.*
>
> You killed something and you killed it when its back was turned

David Levithan

LAW AND ORDER

the judge slams his gavel
and it echoes throughout the
courtroom
it's over
just like that
all those years
and for some strange reason
all I can think of is how you
hated your toast buttered
like why am I thinking about toast
why am I not thinking of when we
met
or when our first child was born
or when we bought our house
toast? really?
who the hell eats dry friggin toast
anyway
it's just so God damn bland
I want to go home and put a pound of
butter on one slice of toast
and then I want to mail it to
you
and hope you choke on it
or even better maybe *she'll*
choke on it
it's breakfast time and I'm craving an
omelet
with peppers and cheese
and Italian toast

heavily buttered, of course
and as I sit at the table
all alone
surrounded by all that deafening
silence
I realize that this may be the best slice of toast
I've ever had

*****One less bell to answer—one less egg to fry***

STAGES OF LOVE

(stage 3—How can I miss you when you never go away)

Jesus Christ
doesn't he know I'm at the friggin
grocery store
I mean give me a break
yea yea, I'll bring home the
beer
and the stupid
potato chips
relax for the love of God
I know it's your poker night
when did he get so
comfortable
and when did I get so
uncomfortable
I just want a minute to
be alone with my thoughts
and maybe a few seconds
alone in the bathroom
and do we really *have*
to make love every morning
and what about the way he
hogs the newspaper
holy shit
maybe I should tell him
I need some space
I feel like a p.o.w.
claustrophobic

but he's such a great guy
I miss him already
omg—is he friggin callin me
again

       ****In the absence of light, you find the
brightest parts of you*

Elvis Bittner

DAZED AND CONFUSED

maybe I was in a
trance
what the hell did I ever
see in him
he was underwhelming
at best
just a lot of
money
but no personality
I needed someone
a *diversion*
someone to fill the
void
and I was a *bitch*
and that was what he
liked
I mean what the hell
for 20 years I kissed someone's
ass and all it got me was
divorced
go figure
so confusing
these games we play
like what was I thinking
as diversions go
he was about a 6
on a 1-10 scale
but I'm over it now
and I'm not dazed or confused

anymore
I just want to be alone
I think it's the best thing for me
cause I'm still in a hundred million
pieces
and I'm not ready to be put back together
just yet

****All the King's horses and all the King's men*
Still can't put me together again
Excerpt from Humpty Dumpty

EGGSHELLS

it's pretty damn
hard
walking on eggshells
tip toeing around
ever so careful not to break
you
carefully weighing every word
that comes out of my
mouth
for fear that you may
crack
or boil over
why is it you think you walk
on water
while I painstakingly
avoid breaking your
ego
I live in fear of
destroying us
when in reality
we have already vaporized
into nothingness

ah those ever resistant
eggshells
not as fragile as one
may think
for you dance on them
and they remain whole
and I would rather smash them

to pieces
than pretend I am not cut by their
fragments

   ***Our love is like an omelet with little bits of*
eggshells in it

AIN'T NO SUNSHINE

even on the cloudiest of
days
I don't miss the sun
there is something about
waiting for that last drop of
rain to fall
or that last cloud to
disappear
that comforts
me
I like to wear sunglasses
when the sun is nowhere to be
found
as if I'm the only one who
can still see ole sol
when in essence I'm just hiding
from the world
pretending that those clouds aren't
ever present
I'm trying so hard to sparkle again
to put the radiance back in my
life
but it's as if every little bit of
brightness
has left me to fend for
myself

and on those darkest of days
I remember

that the sun is usually alone——
but it somehow still manages to
shine

it may take a little while
but I will be a shining star
again
some day when the clouds
leave me behind

****There is no easy way from the earth to the stars*
                                        Seneca

ME AND MY BOO—A DOG NAMED LOU

I'm madly in love with my
dog
he's not a super hero or an
award winning canine
he's just the best dog
ever
he's always so happy to see me
even when I'm a bitch
and he's always ready to snuggle
with me
on any available blanket
he's very intuitive
and I'm pretty sure he can
communicate with the spirits
because he's always just
staring off into space
for hours at a time
he gets very upset if you sit
in his spot
{the big ottoman in the living room}
but he'll never bark at you
after all he's not a jerk
he'll just glare at you until you finally
give up and move
he's very forgiving if I feed him a little late
and he never judges me when I'm a hot mess
hanging in my jammies
havin a glass of wine (or two) with him
I have had lots of friends in my

lifetime
but few have loved me as
unconditionally as Louie
and though he may occasionally
pee on my floor
or scarf a few of my leftovers
I happen to think he's the
cat's ass———and by the way——-
he just loves it when I say that!

***The only fault with a dog is that their lives are too short

SLEEPING WITH THE ENEMY

when did we stop being
lovers
when did the rift between us
become so incredibly
huge
I thought we had a bond
a lifetime promise
but you turned and ran
from everything we were
you ran to her
and now she's the
enemy
and she's like a crack
in our lives
what are you thinking
when you love
me
are you picturing
her
or wishing for
her
and how can you pretend
that we still exist
when there is no us
anymore
Jesus, I wish you would just go
just pack it all in and go
let me sleep one friggin night

without her in the
middle

I don't think you will ever know
what you've truly lost
for I was the best friend you've
ever had
and I am *not* a person you want to have
as an enemy

*****It is a man's own mind, not his enemy, that lures him
to evil ways*

Buddha

WAIT

I spend all my time
waiting
waiting for you to
come back
to where we used to
be
late for dinner
        gone at breakfast
business trips that don't
exist
waiting for you to say
I'm sorry—it was a mistake
waiting for tomorrow
to be a better day
for life to not hurt
and for some sort of
miracle
waiting for healing
and for strength to
forgive
waiting for that bomb
to finally drop

how long can I wait
for the inevitable
break
the end of what was
and the beginning of
what isn't anymore

maybe what I'm waiting for
has already passed
and I'm just waiting
to start over
without you

   ****Let me apologize—I'll make up for all those times.
Wait— Can you turn around?*

Adam Levine—Maroon 5

MELANCHOLY BABY

been in this blue funk
for what seems like an
eternity
somber and gloomy
just plain low
and I don't want to say
it's because of you
that would make this
dismal existence
your fault
and you just don't deserve
that accolade

it's not that I'm depressed
or totally unhappy
it's just like something's
missing
and I'm not even looking for
it
I'm a melancholy baby
nothing's making me
sing
        or rhyme
and I'm really tired of not
smiling so much
but I guess being in the dumps
is better than not
being
at all

and I'm hoping that there's
someone
      somewhere
for me to sing the blues with
and make me his
melancholy baby

      ***Come to me my melancholy baby—cuddle up
and don't be blue
      Written by Ernie Burnett—sung by Ella Fitzgerald

GOOD MORNING, HEARTACHE

it haunts me
now
almost as if
we're friends
just can't shake that
ache
it waits for me at
breakfast
makes its way into my
heart throughout the day
and joins me for a glass of
wine at dinner
that not so subtle pain
that rips into me
like a dose of arsenic
and brings me to my
knees
has become my partner
and companion
offering to keep me company with its
agony
what would I do without it
it's not hard to give in
I make room for it
now
when I remember what used
to be
and I invite it to join me
when I try to sleep

just *please*
stay with me
heartache
you're the only way I know
I'm still alive
I promise to welcome you back
tomorrow
good morning, heartache—sit down

***Might as well get used to you hangin around
Billie Holiday

CLOSE THE DOOR

if I had a nickel
for every time
you left the god damn
door open—
I spent half my days
reminding you to
close the door
behind you
or shut the lights
off
sometimes you'd even forget to close
the car door
and it didn't even bother you
that the friggin alarm went off for
20 minutes
in 15 years you never once
closed the bathroom door
christ that pissed me off
or the garage door
and you wondered why the kids
had their bikes stolen
you left the friggin door open

and here we are
all these years later
and now you decide to
close the door
on us
and here I am

begging you please
leave it open
cause after all this time
I just don't know how
I'll ever find closure
when it was *you*
who finally shut the door

        ***You and I will always be unfinished business*

THE MAGNOLIA TREE

it lived on the front lawn
of the house at 313
majestic in its beauty
it seemed to shelter us
from anything evil
and dad made a ring around the tree
with the blooms
that fell
working them into a sort of
halo
and its beauty
overwhelmed me
and captured a part
of me
and I remember my children
playing by that tree
climbing and jumping
so full of joy
I swear that tree had magical powers
because just inhaling its fragrance
seemed to sooth us
I never wanted to leave
that tree
for its roots run deep
in all of us
those beautiful blossoms
are embedded in our souls
and like its branches
we remain strong

and protected from the
storm

****Trees are poems that the earth writes upon the sky*
                                              Kahlil Gibran

THE GOODBYE GIRL

seems as if I'm always saying
goodbye
to love
or some form of it
and I always have a great excuse
for its departure
the wrong time
        not the right fit
                just wasn't meant to be
love has always been part time
for me
never really had the heart
to hold on to forever
and as far as happily ever after goes
what the hell is that
I always seem to bounce back
though
maybe a little worse for the wear
but it's all good
and the goodbyes get easier
        and easier
as the years roll by
and what was once an insurmountable
loss
barely stings anymore

whenever I wish for love
I remember the inevitable end
and I cringe in anticipation

but more than anything
I wish it could hurt like it
used to
but I know it never will again
cause I'm just too damn good
at goodbyes

****Every time you hurt me the less that I cry and
every time you walk out*
the quicker these tears dry

Sam Smith

SPECIAL VICTIMS

I don't expect any special
treatment
there's nothing exceptional
about your departure
it is what it is
you've gone and left me
again
this may be the millionth time
Jesus, I'm used to it now
I can cope with it now
because it's like any other day
you think I'm special because you broke me
or I'm a victim because I allowed it
it just isn't a big deal
    anymore
it's simply a part of what makes up my world
but what if
    just what if
the axel that balances my world
tilted just a bit
maybe a bit to the left
you might fall off
    and *you* might break
now that would really be something
special
to see you broken and
    to see you as the victim

funny thing about balance
some people have a hard time
with symmetry
and it takes a very special person
to find their balance after a fall
and it takes someone even more special
to bandage the wounds and just
walk away

****Perfect balance is about learning to fall with grace*

PANERA BREAD @ 3 PM

so excited when you called
meeting you for coffee at one of
my favorite places
was going to be the highlight
of my week
you were already there
when I walked in
and I could feel my heart
racing with anticipation
you turned your cheek
when I kissed you
and I knew
something was wrong
it's just not working out
you said
so matter of fact like
    so cold
Jesus, I hope he doesn't say that
but you did
it's me—not you
of course, it's you, you friggin idiot
cause I gave it 150 percent
and it still wasn't enough

and then it was me who turned away
as you walked out the door
and I'm so God damn pissed off
because I love Panera and now I'll never
be able to forget what it stands for

it'll always be the place where you dumped me
and I don't think I'll ever have the appetite
to go back there

goodbye pomegranate muffins
farewell steak paninis
I'll miss you so broccoli cheddar soup in a bread bowl
        life sucks

   ***My weaknesses have always been food and men—in*
that order*

                                        Dolly Parton

A TASTE OF ALONE

I still set the table
use the good dishes
and the best
silverware
pour a glass of
Vina Cobos Felino chardonnay
in my *Mackenzie Childs* glass
and sip the liquid gold
while waiting for the
filet mignon
to cook to perfection
maybe a nice salad
with arugula
and some crumbly gorgonzola
dressed with a lovely
raspberry balsamic
everything's just too perfect
except the table's
set for just one
the chair across from me
remains empty
and echoes of
what used to be
and I still want to savor
the feast I've created with you
I want to see the expression
on your beautiful face
when you realize your steak
is cooked to perfection

but it's dinner for one
again
just another Saturday evening
without you
and I wonder why all this
amazing food
still tastes so good

***I know what I bring to the table, so trust me—I'm not
afraid to eat alone*

A TOAST TO ME

I have a few rules
when it comes to
imbibing—I
never drink alone
or before 5 o'clock
but keep in mind
that I'm never home alone
and it's always 5 o'clock
somewhere
my dog is a great
drinking companion
because he can't argue with me
if I become too opinionated
and he never judges if I've had
one too many
and as for the time
I say it depends on the poison
I mean 3 in the afternoon
may be too early for a Manhattan
but for a lovely grey goose and
cranberry with a splash of lime
on a hot summer day (or any other day)
I say—go for it
and a glass of cabernet always
makes the meal taste better
even if I'm only sharing it with
my dog who by the way prefers a nice *Riesling*
my favorite whine used to be
honey—take me out to dinner

but I've found that when it comes to
the pursuit of happiness
a couple two tree cocktails
can make me just as happy

****Maybe I do drink too much—the last time I gave a urine sample, it had an olive in it*

Rodney Dangerfield

STAGES OF LOVE

(stage 4—it's over)

I'm not saying it will end
not all couples drift apart
I'm in awe of those who live
happily ever after
or ride off into the sunset together
but maybe you should be prepared
stock up on the motrin
and the Xanax
        and the wine
get ready for the pain
and the sleepless nights
just in case your love
bites the dust
been there—done that
get ready for everyone you
run into
to tilt their heads to the side
and ask if you're ok
and even when you say yes
they'll look at you as if you're an
alien with three heads
cause they refuse to believe your legs
weren't shot out from under you
or you're not contemplating suicide
because he's gone
they'll think you're dying inside
and guess what—you are
but you'll get through it—I did

a part of you will never heal
and you may never, ever trust again
but when you think about the good times
you'll be able to smile—because love is always, always
worth the price you have to pay

    ***Why *don't you just pretend that the asshole dropped dead?*

    You can't call or write to a dead man. Put a couple of candles in front of his picture, say a few Hail Mary's, and get it over with."

Irene Lopez

ME MINUS YOU

I come and go exactly as I please
now
don't answer to anyone about anything
and it's funny how the expectations
change
like I know there will be no one home
to help me carry in the groceries
and it doesn't piss me off anymore
cooking is a breeze
when it's only for one
sometimes even a lousy bowl of cereal
is what I have for dinner
but so what—I can eat whatever I want
there's no one but me
controlling the remote
and if I want to watch 36 hours of *Mash*
or *The Godfather* for the 900th time
there's no one bitching about it
at night it's great cause I don't have to
sleep on the left side of the bed
damn—I can sleep sideways in that queen size baby
and it's perfectly ok
but every once in a while, I'm overwhelmed with anger
I'm angry at the world and I hate that it was not my idea
to end it
cause I actually left long before you did
I was somewhere else long before the divorce
but being somewhere else is much different

than being with *someone* else—you sure as hell
proved that

it's Wednesday night and I'm watching a marathon
of all 3 *Godfather* movies
it's nice and cozy in the middle of my bed
got a death grip on the remote
and I'm having a bowl of shredded wheat
and you know what? I'm ok

      ****We told ourselves we had forever and we
never looked back*
              The problem was we never looked ahead
                            Crystal Woods

REVENGE

revenge is what I wanted
pure unadulterated revenge
I wanted him to hurt like the
bastard that he is
like the son of a bitch he was to me
what the hell is the point of trying to be civil
yea—I'm a lady—so what?
so I can't be a bitch, too?
the hell I can't
I can't wish that his {you know what} will fall off
or the ground would open up and swallow his ass
why?
because it's just not the way to handle things
really? Says who?
you think that every woman who's been cheated on
or dumped
or divorced
isn't thinking what I'm thinking?
we all want revenge it's just that some of us are afraid
afraid to say that we hope he rots in hell
well I'm not afraid
he broke me
he took away my breath
my self confidence
my self-worth
        my *dignity*
so you can bet your ass I want revenge
I plan on dancing on his friggin grave
and when revenge finally makes an appearance

on his doorstep
I'm gonna ask him how he likes it
and hope he finally realizes:
karma's a bigger bitch than me

      ***We are never permitted to kill the man who left
us for a younger woman
      But we can take our revenge in the fact that he gets
older every minute

CRAZY

I openly admit I'm a bit
insane at times
it's nothing for me to go from sweet
to total bitch in 1.2 seconds
but I had some help earning this
deranged label
I must have been nuts to ever
trust you and I blame my maniacal obsession
on your lies
and the fact that I became a raving lunatic
when you cheated on me
is a tag I wear with pride
nights alone when I knew you were with her
only made me more of a nut
and the smell of her perfume
totally put me over the edge
insanity is easy to fall prey to
making the same effort over and over
again
and hoping for a different outcome
it's psychotic
and you knew just what buttons to
push
no one can help but go mad
when surrounded only by the essence of
one with a rabid personality
how can one remain sane
when constantly pushed to the limits of
irrational behavior

sure—*I'm a little crazy*
but ask me how I got there and I will be totally
rational when I answer
living with you was like a trip to schizophrenia
and I definitely dropped a few marbles
along the way

　　　***I'm crazy for tryin and crazy for cryin and*
I'm crazy for lovin you

Patsy Cline

SWEAR TO GOD

perhaps I wasn't
a good listener
or maybe I nagged too much
did I sometimes ask too much of you
or turn from your gentle touch
was I too busy with my career
or away from home too often
if this is true I'm sorry love
but I was always near
I swear to God I don't know why
you chose to walk away
nothing has ever changed for me
I can't bear to say goodbye
please turn around and hold me tight
for just a little while
let's try again to work this out
at least for one more night
the mistakes I made were small
compared to the love we shared
can't you change your mind this once
Jesus Christ don't make me crawl
my heart is breaking at the thought of this
I'll never be able to go on
my life is flashing before my eyes
just give me one last kiss
good bye my love I'll miss you so
I don't know what I'll do

I swear to God I'll love you till I die
while I live in your love's afterglow

****No one gets me up there like you can, but boy
you know I'm only human*

Frankie Valli

CINDER F'N RELLA

I mean I'm all for a fairy tale
every once in a while—
who doesn't love a happy ending
but to put my hopes on a peasant girl
who puts all her faith in a fat mouse
and a fairy godmother—come on, really?
and as far as prince frickin charming is concerned
I seriously doubt that he'd chase after some stupid chick
who obviously was too drunk to hold on to her damn shoe
and I have a lot of trouble being able to trust any guy
that runs around in a Nehru jacket and tights—in light blue no less
if I had to relate to anyone in this ridiculous story
I'd be all about the wicked step mom
no wonder she was always pissed off
after all—she hired the girl to clean and cook
and she ends up hanging with a bunch of dirty mice
and what about the wicked step sisters—they really didn't do
anything
Jesus, my sisters are worse than that
and don't even get me started on the stupid glass slipper
who wears glass slippers?? You better have some pretty fabulous
friggin feet and toes to dare and sport something see through on
your feet
pumpkins turning into carriages
        rags into perfectly fitting gowns
                and mice into horses—come on now
I actually believed this crap—
I spent the first 10 years of my life talking to vegetables
and looking for rodents to befriend

it's just too corny for words
anyway—the prince finds his true love—*Cinder f'n rella*
and they ride off together into the sunset on his horse
or was it an oversized mouse
I just find it way too hard to believe—I need reality
something that could actually happen
let's talk *Pretty Woman*
a hooker and a billionaire—yup—my kind of story
happens every day—right?

> ***Big deal—so Cinderella walked on broken glass***
>
> I've always known the right shoes could change someone's life

THROUGH THE FIRE

our love
was a bright red ember that was never supposed
to burn out
flames of passion that would last forever
evenings filled with shooting stars
and wishes made on crescent moons
we were loves' towering inferno
a perpetual campfire that warmed our souls
ever burning with desire
      always in the midst of a sea of flames
but anything fueled by fire burns out too quickly
and like so many lovers before us
there was nothing left but the ashes
the dust of what was
      cinders of two used to be lovers
that melted into ice
we were through before we started
no more me and you

I stare into the flames of the fire
prodding the pieces of wood
with the iron rod
sparks fly and singe my very soul
and I'm desperately trying to keep the fire
alive, but
it's just about out now
ashes cold and lifeless
and I wonder if those flames that used to wear

our names
will ever burn so brightly again

      ****Through the fire to the limit to the wall, for*
just a chance to be with you
         I'd gladly risk it all

                  Chaka Khan

BAD TO THE BONE

gotta love those bad
boys
those nasty guys that make us
swoon
lie after lie that we take as
gospel
and even though we know
we're being used and abused
we just keep going back for more
they can stand us up
    cheat
         disappear for days at a time
and we'll open the door and welcome
them back
right now you're picturing
the *James Dean* type
a black leather jacket
and a motorcycle
maybe a few tats
but what about that bad boy
in the double-breasted suit
carrying a *Louis Vuitton*
valise
who can bring you to your
knees
with just a look from his
deep set green eyes
and you think he's all that
and a bag of chips

but *guess what?*
so does his wife
bad to the bone

I'll make a rich woman beg, make a good woman steel
make an old woman blush and make a young girl squeal
        B B B bad to the bone
                George Thorogood—The Destroyers

YOU—TALKIN TO ME?

I finally realized the number of faces
you show to the public in all sorts of places
the lies and the hurt that spew from your lips
it must be Satan that's writing your scripts
your ego is something the size of an acre
and you fancy yourself a real heartbreaker
you think that this world revolves around you
and you just can't believe I'm sayin we're through
don't talk to me about breaking your heart
cause you never had one to break from the start
your evil and hurtful and incapable of love
and you know that description fits like a glove
you never deserved the love that I gave
and now I know there's nothin to save
don't talk at all cause I don't want to hear
you lying and sayin you still want me near
don't tell me you love me when I know it's not true
cause the only person you've ever loved is you
just walk out the door and don't say a thing
I'm no longer your puppet— I'm cuttin the strings
someday you'll realize just what you had
cause I was the best of the best and it's sad
and when you're alone and you're cold and afraid
remember it was you and not me that strayed
from a love that was destroyed by all that you did
I hope it kills you—cause you deserve it, kid
and I'll be just fine without you I know
I'll be stronger and happy and continue to grow
but you'll never change cause you think you're so cool

you're nothing my friend just a stupid old fool
you threw us away for younger, greener grass
good riddance you jerk—you're just not in my class!

    ***Talk, talk, talk—the utter stupidity and heartbreak of words*

William Faulkner

LIKE A MOTH TO A FLAME

I don't know what drew me to you
maybe your sense of humor
I've always been a sucker for a guy
who could make me laugh
or maybe it was your eyes
as blue as the sky
that put me under your spell
you are a magician
and I have disappeared into
you
like a falling star I pray you'll
catch me
and keep me until I fade away
for I have become what I never thought I would
just a captive child who clings to your every word
a prisoner who wants no freedom
and like a moth to the flame
I am helpless
and I willingly surrender

maybe tomorrow you'll be gone
and I will be the fool
but today I am smack dab in the middle
of love
and there's nowhere else I can be
but with you

*** *You are and always have been—my dream*
Noah—from The Notebook

                                        Nicholas Sparks

G CLEF

welcome to the orchestration of
my life
and on those days when I am full of
myself and happiness prevails
I inhale the sounds of the piano
with just a taste of the licorice stick
and when I am feeling flirtatious
I surround myself in those sexual sounds
of the saxophone with just a touch of a risqué
trombone
sometimes angelic I am lost in the beauty of the
harp
totally engrossed in the perfection of its strings
with maybe a touch of a viola humming in vibrato
and oh the prideful vanity of the drum
fills me with confidence and aplomb
marching to its beat as if it were my job
I may occasionally be under a cloud
covered with the blanket of a cello
low and comforting and full of promise
but you
    you are the maestro
and I am but a tiny instrument of your
symphony
and you play me for all to hear
in the sweetest possible notes

composed for me alone
and our duet can be heard
around the world
for we are more than harmonious
we are the music of love

> ***Music is my life—it is a reflection of what I go through***
>   Lenny Kravitz

BLACK SWAN

in a crystal-clear pond
full of their own
reflection
swim the purest white
swans
graceful and elegant
for all the world to
admire
they are perched so majestically as if to say
we are royalty—the fairest of our species
yet in the midst of these genteel creatures
floats the most eye catching of all
covered in velvet feathers as black as
night
and alone in its beauty so reverent
demanding no one look elsewhere
submerged in the pond looking almost
statuesque
this swan of color beckons all that stare
demanding respect and adoration
and I am in awe of the silk-like texture
of its graceful neck and body
as it overtakes the hidden lagoon

I imagine that if I were a swan
I would be that black swan
ever so mysterious in nature
perhaps igniting a bit of trepidation
in those who dare to approach

for like the color it boasts
I prefer the raven-like personality
of the onyx beauty
overstated and daunting
like the darkness in my soul

****It's such a beautiful day out—I think I'll wear black*

STORMY WEATHER

it's hard to be stronger
than the storm
fighting the tempest that seems
to follow me
the clouds open up and attempt
to swallow all that I am
and I continue to battle this war of
life
enemies approach and threaten to
destroy
what I have fought so hard to
accomplish
hatred and damnable opponents
attempt to strip me of my
very being
and I cling to my integrity
as if it were an umbrella
and yes—I have rocked the
boat
more times than most people would
dare
yet I did not drown
nor did I surrender
to the storm
and as I continue to fight
this onslaught of hatred
and jealousy and envy
I am only more substantial
and tenacious

for I am fighting for my very
life
and the right to be
the woman I have become

****Don't know why there's no sun up in the sky*
Etta James

AT MY AGE

at my age
I should know better
I shouldn't let things upset me
why do I bother to put make up on
just to go to the grocery store
why do I cook so much
why am I still working
when all my friends are retired
why do I find polyester so
offensive
and why the hell shouldn't I have
a sugar daddy
why do my children think
they are my parents now
and you can bet your ass
I'll never be a fan of the Kardashian
family
at this age
I shouldn't dress the way I do
and I'm supposed to like
knitting or some sort of
needle work
and watch my language
because I'm just too old for
that bullshit
age is just a number
just a digit of sorts
this is the age I have
waited for

the age of awakening
and I am more than comfortable
in my own skin
and being who I am
at my age

***The older I get the more I feel almost beautiful*

WHITE BREAD

he was white bread
    milk toast
so boring
let me explain
when I sink my teeth into anything
it's got to have some substance—some grit
you know—a nice crusty offering
with a soft middle
like a delicious *ciabatta*
or even a lovely *focaccia*
I've got to have something
that bites back
and a wonder bread man
isn't gonna cut it
I mean it's like making an incredible meatball
all soft and gooey dripping with all that
homemade sauce
and then putting it between two pieces of
white bread with mayo——

    I could never love a man who does that
life is bread
    it's like a communion of sorts
we need bread to be the core of our relationships
a beautiful chewy loaf that stands up
to all we put between it
to me—life is all about the nourishment of
that amazing deliciousness that at its best
fills our home with the aroma of love
and even at its worst can feed us

when we have nothing else
as I savor my feast
of capicola, lettuce and tomato
nestled between two slices of warm *Italian* bread
I imagine *it* is out there
that one perfect loaf of scrumptiousness
baked to perfection and waiting
for my indulgence

***How can a nation be great if its bread tastes like Kleenex?
                                        Julia Childs

SLOW BOAT TO CHINA

let's get away
he said
maybe a nice slow boat
to China
wouldn't that be lovely
and I thought I would faint
at the thought of that trip
where has this man been for the last
20 years
does he not know that I don't do boats
or China
the only China I am even remotely interested in
is a dinner plate by *Lenox*
good lord—China—ugh
take me to Paris or Rome
indulge me with a weekend in New York
pamper me on Rodeo Drive
but China—pass
and a slow boat
I'm petrified of slow anything
cause I'm a fast movin kinda gal
and he wants to get me on a slow boat
to china
I'd rather go on a picnic
and anyone that knows me
knows I hate picnics more than
anything—all that nature can kill you
so let's revamp this slow boat
thing

how bout leaving on a jet plane
we'll do New York—dinner at Bobby Flay's
maybe drinks at Mario Batali's
shopping at Bloomingdales—
honey—I'm packed and ready to fly

***The song says—"Fly me to the Moon"—not sail me to it

IN THE MOOD

I am in the mood
for you
morning noon and night
you are my craving
     my temptation
          my persuasion
you laugh and I feel alive
your smile is my favorite drug
taking me higher than I ever thought
possible
and your kiss can melt me as if I were
ice on a hot flame
I am always in the mood for your embrace
whether it be just the touch of
your cheek
or falling into your open arms
I am helpless
     hopelessly intoxicated
by you
     with you   about you
my mood is dependent upon
you
dismal and blue when you are away
my heart hardly dares to beat
until you resuscitate me
I am always in the mood
my love
for you are pleasure and affection
you are bliss

you are my favorite distraction
you are *love*

   ***I'm in the mood for love—simply because you're near me
Funny but when you're near me—I'm in the mood for love

COMPARED TO WHAT

it was a million years
ago
when you walked away
and never looked back
and I hear you're happy
yet I can't move on
they say I'm better off
compared to what
compared to the pain
        or the heartache
that still engulfs me
compared to the overwhelming
loneliness that surrounds me
night after night
I compare your departure to
winter
it's like being frozen in time
numb and indifferent
it's as if I am the walking
dead
paralyzed and apathetic
incapable of living as before
and knowing there is no return
from this torment

I carefully analyze everyone I meet
searching for that certain something
I saw in you
maybe a glimmer of hope in a stranger's

eyes
or a spark of optimism in the starlight
but it has become unquestionably true
nothing in this world
compares to you

    ***Happiness is not an absolute value. It is a state
of comparison

Zadie Smith

THROUGH THE LOOKING GLASS

at the risk of sounding a bit
egotistical
I used to enjoy gazing at myself
in the mirror
spending a few minutes admiring my face
maybe giving myself a pat on the back
for not gaining any weight
even though I inhaled almost an entire pizza
the night before
I liked what I used to see
but things are a bit different now
the mirror is no longer my friend
I have come to the conclusion—-*it lies*
along with several other inaccurate
appliances like my scale and blood pressure cuff
running past the mirror is an everyday occurrence
but as long as I'm able to zip my pants
and I'm not sporting a moustache
I'm good to go
I just don't understand why the mirror
has to be so cruel
it can't be possible that I'm this age
that my skin is starting to wrinkle and sag
the youthful glow I once wore
has been replaced by the sallow
look of one along in years
friggin mirrors—I've replaced the one in
my bedroom three times yet
they are all defective

perhaps Alice had the right idea
I need to go through the looking glass
I'm pretty sure my youth
is waiting on the other side

****When you talk to a mirror say only two words: Hello
Beautiful!*

Richelle Goodrich

HAPPY ENDINGS

do you believe in fairy tales
I'd really like to know
cause I can't seem to understand
why love always has to fail
what about the princess bride
who always gets her man
no matter what he has to do
he takes it all in stride
and what about that piece of fruit
they fed to poor snow white
it almost killed the virgin girl
that fact we can't dispute
sleeping beauty took a hit
from a spinning needle no less
that put her in a glass coffin
for too many years, I admit
for me there never was a prince
or men to rescue me
I've always been the one with the frogs
so I may be hard to convince
that there's such a thing as forever
or even 20 years
but if you can make me understand
it'll be my next endeavor
I'll advertise in tomorrow's paper
prince wanted: apply within
and then I'll wait so patiently
in the highest of high skyscrapers
and if he finds me way up here

just waiting with my head in the clouds
I'll gladly believe in forever and a day
and my doubts will all disappear
farewell you ugly frogs and toads
I'm a princess now, take heed
I'm finally a believer in a happy ending
——stay tuned for the next episode!

****I admit I've never met prince charming—but prince terrifying—we're old friends*

BROKEN

I know you're broken
and I'm sorry
I wish I could fix you
put the pieces back together
but I can't
I can't glue you back to the way
you were
you need to do that alone
but I can help you
rebuild yourself and
become an even better version
of who you used to be
I can reassure you of your talents
and your strengths
I will remind you that you are capable
of anything
I have seen you crumble into the dirt
wanting only to remain dormant
but I can't let you do that
I can't let the mud swallow you
because you deserve so much more
and I will believe in you forever and a day
because you are so much more than
you can see right now
you are the light at the end of the tunnel
and the prize at the end of the hunt
you are a rainbow after the storm
and the silver lining to the clouds
I will be behind you when you think you might fall

and I will be your laughter when you can only cry
and when you are no longer broken
I will help you stand tall
for there will always be other wars
you will have to fight
but never forget that I will be there to hand you the weapons
I will be with you even after death
until all your battles have been won
and you are finally the victor

      ****Want to know if I have connections?? Hurt one of my children!*

MILLION DOLLAR BABY

I'm sad for you
sad because you never took the time
to know the real me
and maybe a bit miffed since you are still
totally unaware of the loss
I am so much more than a pretty face
so much more than arm candy
I'm funny and smart
        sensitive and intuitive
and though I'm sometimes biased
when it comes to my family
I'm faithful—at least I was to you
and I love deeply and without
reservation
you could never appreciate my talents
never took an interest in my thoughts
or involvements
it was always just about you

and after you left
I finally realized
that I was all these things
and more
more than you ever wanted me
to be
I am one in a million
and I am proud of all I've
accomplished
I was never your idea

of the perfect woman
I doubt such a woman exists
but I am so much more
than you will ever, ever know
and I am so happy for me
because I am worth every last penny
of the million-dollar baby
you never bothered to know

      ***I found a million-dollar baby in a five and ten cent store*
        Written by Billy Rose—sung by Bing Crosby

IT HAD TO BE YOU

happy being miserable
with you
was better than nothing
you were *the one*
you were supposed to be my
happily ever after
we were going to be that couple
that still held hands when we were 80
the couple that beat all the odds
madly in love for 75 years
it was always you
and even now when I hear your name
the memories wash over me
and I still have to fight to stay
afloat
even now when there's someone else
it hurts to think of the broken promises
and you in the arms of another
I only hope that he will never know
that you still haunt my dreams
and that a part of me will never heal

I am comfortable now
he's made us a good life
yet I long for the passion
only you could stir
and deep down in my soul
it's still you and me
cause it was only you

that could make me beyond happy
when all you gave me was misery

****Nobody else gave me a thrill—with all your faults I love you still*
It had to be you, wonderful you—it had to be you
Harry Connick, Jr.

WEEKEND IN GENEVA

a much needed get away
just me and my thoughts
no intentions of meeting
anyone
much less staying for a
weekend
but there you were
alone like me
two strangers thrown together
by fate
a couple of cocktails
led to a few more
and a walk along the lake
pretending we had no secrets
afraid to tell the truth
and yet somehow finding comfort
as we continued the masquerade
just a weekend in Geneva

we said good bye already clinging
to the memories
somehow knowing those memories
would have to sustain us
I watched as you drove away
And hoped you'd remember me
and the walk along the water
and I looked to the sky to capture

a shooting star
and named it after you

***I'm back in the city where nothing seems clear—
But thoughts of you holding me bringing me near
Barry Manilow

BLOOD LINES

on those dismal days
when I want to stay in bed
and just give up
I remember
it's not in my blood
I fight to survive
and sometimes just to
breathe
because it's how I was
raised
a warrior
    a soldier
taught to put aside hatred
and thoughts of
revenge
it was almost satanical to
wish any foreboding acts
to our enemies
it's not in my blood
but you crippled me
pieces of me remain fragmented
and lost
shattered like glass
and try as I may to recover
to reconstruct my person
I can't
    I just can't
you are in my blood
like life's sustenance

you flow through me
and I cannot live
without you

     ***He was both everything I could ever want—and
nothing I could ever have

                    Ranata Suzuki

FOOL ME ONCE

once upon a time
a million years ago
I let you fool me
the deception was easy
for I was blinded by love
and it was like leading the lamb
to slaughter
the lies flowed from your lips
like sweet poetry
and I savored every delicious word
until I was saturated with so much
delusion
that I could no longer ingest the
deceit
and the trust I gave you
was destroyed
like so many of love's old adages
and I became numb
    and frozen
and your words could no longer
permeate
and I was nobody's fool anymore

I survived your fraudulence
but you'll never know the price
I paid
nothing can penetrate me now
I am a hardened shell
wiser by far

but ever foolish when I remember
you

      ****I just wanted to be your fool—but you were*
too much a fool to understand

Arzum Azun

IF I DIDN'T CARE

lying awake at night
I remember
how the window had to be open
just a little bit
and it was so damn cold
but it was what you wanted
and I remember how your coffee
had to be warm—not hot
with brown sugar because it was better
for you
it was ok that we never watched those old
Fred Astaire movies
or *Mary Tyler Moore*
because watching football while lying in
your arms was all I needed
and I cared enough to forget about the first
indiscretion
but I had a more difficult time
with the second
     and third
and I would iron your shirts
still fragrant with her perfume
even after being washed
and pretend I couldn't smell
the odor of infidelity
and I cared enough to let you go
because it was what you said you needed
to be happy

here we are
2 years later
and you're begging me
to let you come home
but I can't do that
cause I've finally moved on
and I just don't care
anymore

     ***I have come to believe that caring for myself is
not self-indulgent
     It is an act of survival
               Audre Lorde

OFF THE MENU

how great would it be
if love had a menu
I could place an order
for the perfect companion
        or the perfect lover
one from column A
        two from column B
blue eyes or brown eyes
tall or not so tall
I wonder if the order would be
standard
and if you would need to special order things like
empathy and tenderness
unselfishness and kindness
that would be ala carte
and I'm sure that would be much more
expensive
and what if I wanted this special-order man
to stay for quite a while
would I pay by the week
or rent daily
I'd have to be able to send him back
if he wasn't to my liking
after all—no one keeps a steak if it's overcooked
and I sure wouldn't pay for him
if he were spoiled or too tuff
I mean if I'm paying—he's got to be perfect
right?
a menu for love

    what a novel idea
tonight's Saturday and I'm in the mood
for tall dark and rich
with a side of sexy and well dressed
so I'm gonna order out

I just hope they deliver——
cause I've never been
a *pick-up* kinda gal!

                  ****Let's just hope if I pay $300 for*
takeout—I won't be hungry again in an hour

THE DAY AFTER

the alarm goes off
as usual
hot shower
    light breakfast
uneventful drive to work
maybe stop for a latte
at Starbucks
9 – 5 grind
everything is just as it was
except
every few minutes
this never-ending reality
washes over me
you're gone
lunch is the same
salad and water with lemon
joke with my co-workers
annoyed with the public
and here it comes again—-*I'm alone*
lots of traffic on the way home
display just a bit of road rage
let the dog out and start dinner
dinner for one—cocktails for one
but enough hurt to fill a small planet
anything to stay up a little longer
just too hard to face the empty bed
and I've done everything in my power
to pretend I'm ok but I'm not
it's the day after my life ended

I don't feel as if I'm even alive
so how do I get through the day
without you
why isn't everything changing
or time standing still
I am not the same
so why won't the world make the adjustment
just set the stars on a different path
and make it yesterday again

****Why should I let go of yesterday? Because yesterday already let go of you!*
Steve Maroboli

DINNER FOR ONE

I choose the best restaurant in town
make an eight o'clock reservation
and slip into a sexy little black dress
strappy red pumps and a spray of
Chanel
I'm ready
the waiter asks if anyone will be joining me
"No" I say and smile my brightest smile
I order my favorite dish
and an ice cold cosmopolitan
straight up
and try not to think about the fact that
I'm eating alone
    I'm having dinner for one
my ears feel as if they're on fire and people are staring
God, this is hard
I close my eyes for just a moment
hoping that when I open them
you'll be sitting across from me
nope—still alone
and suddenly I'm inundated with memories
of every dinner we've ever had together
the appetizers and the desserts
the drinks and the conversations
and I am astutely aware of my
singleness
I order another Cosmo
and sip it slowly
and say yes to the man

who asks to buy me a cocktail
cause no one says I have to drink
alone, too

       ****They're sharing a drink they call loneliness—*
but it's better than drinking alone

Billy Joel

SCARS

a lot of them have been mended
already
not painful at all anymore
got a few that really
left a mark
and will probably never heal
but they're easier to hide
now
some of them are still
fresh
even though it's been years
sometimes just a memory can
open them again
and they'll bleed
like it just happened
my heart's been pieced back together
a million times
maybe it's not as receptive as it used to be
but hey——-I'm still alive
hell—some of the scars I'm damn proud of
especially those that should have killed me
but I survived
no thanks to love
        or commitment
so what you see is far from perfect
maybe you won't see the breaks
or notice the defects
but you will feel the difference
if you fall for me

cause I'll never let you get close enough
to leave another scar

      ****I wear my scars the way some women wear
their finest jewels*

ALL ABOUT ME

it's finally all about me
now
I can do whatever I want
    whenever I want
        with whomever I want
no one to cook for
or buy cards for
and who do I tell those deep dark
secrets to
there's no one to hold me
in the middle of the night
and no one to dry my tears
after I watch *The Way We Were*
for the 10 thousandth time
who will tell me I'm beautiful
or funny or lie to me when I ask:
does this make me look fat
and who will fight me for that last bite
of chocolate cake
who do I run to if I'm sad or upset
and when I'm just not feeling well
who will bring me flowers and
lemon cough drops
who can I text at 3 am when I'm wide awake
or call when I first awaken just to say hello
and who will tell me they love me
just before bed
or kiss my forehead as if I were a child

it's all about me
now
as I search for things to fill the void
and I remember when it used to be
all about us
and I wrap myself in those memories
and hope I see you
just one more time
in my dreams

> ***I'll let you be in my dreams if I can be in yours*
> Bob Dylan

THE PERFECT STORM

you were the perfect storm
a little hurricane mixed with
a touch of a tropical breeze
a whirlwind romance
that left me searching for the
rainbow
dormant for a while
but always followed by a
cloudburst
sometimes frightening
in its severity
but always exciting
and full of passion
you were thunder and lightening
a tender cyclone
that drenched me with rain
a brilliant tempest
that warmed like a gentle breeze
a God in the midst of a typhoon

how could I have known
that sunshine could be cold
that the aftermath of you
would be like frost in the summer
that the calm after the storm
would leave me longing for rain

and now when I hear thunder
I stand in the middle of the storm

alone with no umbrella
and search for you

       ****You fell in love with a storm—did you think
you would get out unscathed?*
Nakita Gill

WHEN THE LIGHTS GO OUT

I'm so much braver
in the dark
waves of black cover me
and I come alive
flaws disappear
and scars vanish
and I am only who I
wish to be
imagination rules
and I am invincible
I am yours
dreams dance and come to life
and I am in control
not even the stars
can outshine me
and I bask in the obscurity
of night
the crescent moon sheds just enough light
to pave my way
into the shadows of fantasy
and I am one with the darkness

and as the twilight breaks
it is me that fades
and the sunlight burns me into
reality
and beckons me awake
and I will pretend for another day
to be at peace with the light

"Now not day only shall be beloved, but night too shall be beautiful and blessed and all its fear pass away."

J.R.R. Tolkien

SATURDAY NIGHT FEVER

God—-I used to love Saturday nights
dressed to kill
armed with passion and lies
perfectly made up
hair teased to about a mile high
lips plumped and painted bright pink
full of hope for what might be
hoping to find true love or lust
ready to make a grand entrance
and searching for new talent
at the same old haunts
scotch on the rocks
lipstick stained glasses
long white tipped cigarettes
and boys pretending to be men
music so loud there was no need to converse
and slow dances that promised what would never be
delivered
like dust the lies flew
and made us believers
and followers
of our dreams
as we pretended to be
someone else
    something different
but we all wanted the same thing
we all believed the same lies

we burned with fever on those Saturday nights

full of hope and rapture
naïve and innocent
still unscathed by loves cruelty
and hopeful for tomorrow

we never found what we were looking for
not there—not at those too familiar places
but it made for unforgettable memories
and paved our way to reality

****Would ya just watch the hair!! I spend a lot of time on the hair—don't hit it!*
John Travolta—Saturday Night Fever

DIVORCE ANYONE?

it's like the loss of a limb
you survive, but there's less of you
it's about as painful as dying
and as long lasting as eternity
it's waking in the morning and
realizing all over again that you're alone
and it's like a sort of dementia
because even if you forget it for a while
it slaps you in the face with its reality
it takes you away from everything you once knew
and steers you into stuff you never dreamed you'd want
it's settling for defeat and it's change—irrevocable change
and it shreds the muscles of your heart so that it hardly beats
it's like wearing a sign that screams *"person going through a
divorce"*
and the whole world seems tilted—off center—wrong
love turns to hate and hate to indifference
and you begin to trivialize your entire life
it's owning terminology you hate
like—-*broken marriage or unhappy household*
and everything that used to be together is
broken, shattered, destroyed
it's a macabre way of life—an earth-shattering loss
and it's a constant state of pretending
it's letting go when you don't want to and
forcing yourself to start over
it's a river of tears—-lots and lots of tears
you literally cry an ocean and then
you want to drown yourself *or him* in it

but somehow you survive
it's every sad movie you've ever seen
and every God damn sad love song
and it just plain hurts like a bitch
and when they whisper *"She's divorced"*
I simply look up at them and smile
because sometimes love is not everlasting
sometimes it's just for a while
and I've moved on—took another road
because if I didn't—life would have run me over

****Sometimes divorce is the best thing that can happen to marriage*

MOONGLOW

we all have our dark side
like the moon
and sometimes when I'm taking in its beauty
I imagine how the stars must feel
surrounded by all that exquisiteness
maybe they are sometimes fearful
of that inky imperfection
for even the moon in all its glory
has been compared to lunacy
the moon never hangs quite the same
and some people are frightened by its ever-changing silhouette
and its flirtatious lavender color
but I am a lover of that ever-present sphere
of its brilliance and radiance
I love how it seems to shine just for me
and how in its crescent shape it still awakens the child in me
as I search for the proverbial cow jumping so high in the sky
I love the way it can sing to us of love and guide our way in the
evening
and how so many of us have been almost bruised by its beauty
after we tell our deepest secrets to the man who lives there
and I always remember in my loneliest times as I stare at the full
moon
that someone else somewhere is staring at it too
looking at the same perfection
maybe someone like me
another lover of this poetic orb
and as the moon romances us to sleep

it spills its silver lining on our hearts
and promises to shine again tomorrow

***On a clear night, the moon and the stars are enough

SLEEPWALK

arms outstretched
running towards your silhouette
I know it's a dream
but it's so real
I want to hold you
just one more time
to stay in your arms for just a little while
to feel your kiss and the warmth of your lips
my legs are heavy with anticipation
as I struggle to reach you
I feel as if I'm screaming your name
but I am surrounded by silence
and you won't turn around
I'm dreaming
and then as if I were no longer asleep
you're holding me
and telling me it's ok
and I inhale the scent of linen and ocean
that was always you
waves of euphoria lift me to another level
and I hang on for dear life
and you're telling me to stay
and I want to
I so want to
I feel a pull and I'm startled awake
I can still see you and taste the salt from your lips
my pillow is damp and smells like the ocean
but you are not here
like every other night— I am alone

I will learn to sleepwalk
and my days will be spent in anticipation
of the evening
where we can blissfully slip into dreamland together
sleepwalking backwards into love again

****I am hypnotized. Sleepwalking to the rhythm
of your words never wishing to wake*
Michael Faudet

STAGES OF LOVE

(stage 5, starting over)

it's almost inevitable
bound to happen
you're out on an ordinary Friday night
and there he is
he's sipping on a vodka martini alone at the bar
and he offers to buy you a drink
and you think: *why the hell not*
he's charismatic as all get out
smells great—nicely dressed—easy on the eyes
no wedding band
the conversation just flows
so much in common
and you give him your number
he walks you to your car
tells you he'll call and kisses you good night

you're up all-night tossing and turning
I wonder when he'll call
do you really want to start something again
you're just crawling out from under the black cloud
where you've lived for the past 6 months
and you're thinking: *is it worth it?*
but you can't get him off your mind
a couple of days drag by and still no call
no way in hell am I gonna call him
now it's Friday morning and he shoots you a text
wanna catch a movie tonight
man—he's got a set of balls! Where does he get off thinking I'm

available on such short notice?
so you see a foreign film and then dinner and drinks
sex at your apartment and guess what?
you're smack dab back in the thick of it

it's a week later—still no call. *I must be insane*
welcome to that old familiar feeling, girl!
ain't love a kick in the head??!!

       ***Don't let the devil fool you—unless he's*
handsome!
      and then, remember——fools rush in!

AT THE END OF MY ROPE

how much longer did you think I could
hang on?
how much more could I take?
you pushed me so far away there was no
turning back
no recovery
years of neglect and loneliness
forced me into a bitter existence
and though they say ignorance is bliss
nothing could be further from the truth
eye-opening reality hits like a heavyweight
and it's tuff to get up after being knocked down so many times
blankets of lies
night after sleepless night in a pit of solitude
while you embraced slumber like a new born babe
and my hands are still bruised from holding on to a rope of thorns
bloody from trying not to let go
of you
    of us

and I didn't just walk away
    I ran
into another hell maybe even worse than the one you created
a purgatory of sorts where I'm repenting for *your* sins
a dark abyss that reminds me of how I got here
day after miserable day
and while you wallow in your own creation of nirvana
I'm still trying to hang on to that rope—to regain my footing

but it's so friggin hard to climb back up to the top
when you've been pinned down at the bottom for so long

   ***It's painful and it's messy. But sometimes you just
have to make the break and start again***
              Tony Parsons

EAT, PRAY, LOVE

indulge in daily feasts
eat as if it's your last meal
have that second piece of cake
eat with total abandonment and toast to life
cook as if you're Julia Childs or Ina Garten and make every dish
a work of art dripping with your own personal spice
take a step back and admire your creation
then lick your lips and dig in—-savor each and every bite

pray for forgiveness
pray for health and happiness
pray for those less fortunate than you
for those that are lonely—-and for those in pain
pray to be a better person
and pray again for forgiveness
remember none of us are perfect
but there is power in prayer and remember
you are deserving of something miraculous

love like it's your first time
love with your heart and soul
with your head and your entire being
love even when you don't like anything
and love those that hate
love as if it's your job
as if it's what you were put on this earth for
and most of all love yourself
embrace your faults and your accomplishments
learn to love life's bad days and good days

and love what you've been blessed to receive
let go of what was not meant to be
and remember what worked yesterday might not work today
love is food for the soul
    eat pray love
and live like there's no tomorrow

    ***Love is an eternal first breath*
    To become bored with eating is to be bored with life
    Do not pray for an easy life. Pray for the strength to
endure a difficult one
EAT PRAY LOVE

SAD SONGS

there is something about a
sad love song
something that can bring me to my
knees
almost makes me feel faint
when that rush of memories
fills my head
note after painful note
opens the wounds
again
and the scars
are fresh
like it just
happened
with each verse
you return to
me
with each chorus
you are here
and I ingest the
song
as if it were a
drug
hypnotic and
mesmerizing
it is perhaps 3
minutes of bliss
3 minutes of
torture

but the song plays for
us
like before
when the music was ours
and the melody was love
and now it plays for
someone else
who will really never understand
the words

*****Take my hand take my whole life, too. Cause
I can't help falling in love with you*
Elvis Presley

THE WEATHER OF LOVE

love has the strangest way
of showing up when we least
expect it
it can make a flower blossom
or wilt like a weed
it can be a beast
in the form of beauty
and it can be perfection
disguised as evil
love can be an olive branch
or a dandelion
it can surface in the midst of a storm
or laugh at the sunshine
it can make you weep when you want to laugh
or die a thousand times a day

never fall for someone
who will only love you
under favorable conditions
but love the one
who will dance with you
in the rain
love the one that will make love
bloom
and nurture you
as he would a small child
surrender to loves
unpredictability
as you would a change in

the weather
wear a raincoat if you must
but never, ever expect it to be sunny
every day
love is a turbulence
hang on
for there will be hail
but love will always be greater
when you brave the elements
together

****Weather is unrehearsed—like true love*

EPILOGUE

Just because this book is about failed love, don't think for one minute that I am not a believer. I think falling in love and staying in love with the same person is all that and a bag of chips. For me, it was just not meant to be—but not for lack of trying!

To say I made bad choices would be an understatement. My marriages were based more on infatuation than love. As I look back, I remember feeling almost "giddy" with anticipation of what was to come. I was focused on a fairy tale existence, much too immature to embrace the true worth of marriage and the never-ending responsibilities that marriage needs to grow and survive. I was still convinced that the world owed me something—along with every man I met. I needed top billing and usually got it.

If you search the dictionary for the term "Late Bloomer" you will surely find my picture—though I'm sure I still haven't reached some editions. I am yet undecided as to why I took so long to grow up, and I'm sure some people would argue I am still not quite as "mature" as I should be for a woman well up in years. I still delight in the purchase of an expensive pair of shoes and it is only in the last 15 years that I decided paying bills should come before spoiling myself. Needless to say, I spent a lot of time chasing my own tail.

Ah—but what about love. Never think for one moment I haven't experienced what the poets write about. I have been hit by the thunderbolt more times than I care to admit and have willingly and unwillingly experienced all the best (and worst) symptoms of the magnificent obsession. Sleepless nights, loss of appetite (I always favored that one—might as well loose a few pounds), butterflies in the stomach, sweaty palms (not one of my favorites) and that all time winner—first time jitters. Gotta love it! There is nothing like love—I highly recommend it!

The love of my three children is almost too intense for me to explain. It is a love that I have always embraced and administered with the utmost pleasure and without reservation. To experience the love of a child is to me, a miracle. And to watch them grow and become parents and responsible adults is nothing short of amazing. My children are selfless and loyal—traits that come much more from my family than me personally. I am beyond proud of each and every one of them. They are beautiful inside and out and anyone who doesn't believe in miracles has only to look at a child to have a mind-altering experience! That love only intensifies when you are blessed with grandchildren. I happen to have four of the best. They are loving and kind and in my opinion; brilliant, talented and exceptionally good looking—qualities they no doubt inherited from me.

Fall in love—over and over again. Love unconditionally and with sheer abandonment. Love as if it's your last day on earth. Never expect to be unscathed by this passion. Accept it as you would any other everyday occurrence—like the sunshine or the rain or a broken limb. Remember that you will have good days and bad days and that love will find you in the worst of times. Embrace it. As many times as love has left me wounded and bruised, I hope with all my heart it will find me again. And I'm ready for it this time. This time I will accept it for what it is. *An imperfect perfection.* A blessing. A commitment. A son of a bitch to control and a miracle. I am waiting. This time I am not expecting Prince Charming nor do I want him. If I am blessed to find someone at this stage of my life, I hope only that he is kind and loving. That he will have as strong a devotion to family as me. And that he can accept my flaws—because there are quite a few. I pray for an imperfect romantic that will still be able to teach this old gal a few tricks and that together we can share a comfort and acceptance that we've both earned. I wish for a believer—just like me. And though you may not find it in the pages of this book, I wish for each and every one of you to be blessed with a love like you read about. A happily ever after love. A fairy tale of sorts and a happy ending. Because when the smoke clears and we look back on our yesterdays—love is what made it all happen. To the dream makers, the true believers, the forever and a day crowd and those whose commitments have weathered the test of time, I salute you! And I wish for all of you a continuance of God's most valued miracle—Love!

Marianne

Only once in your life, I truly believe, you find someone who can completely turn your world around. You tell them things that you've never shared with another soul and they absorb everything you say and actually want to hear more. You share hopes for the future, dreams that will never come true, goals that were never achieved and the many disappointments life has thrown at you. When something wonderful happens, you can't wait to tell them about it, knowing they will share in your excitement. They are not embarrassed to cry with you when you are hurting or laugh with you when you make a fool of yourself. Never do they hurt your feelings or make you feel like you are not good enough, but rather they build you up and show you the things about yourself that make you special and even beautiful. There is never any pressure, jealousy or competition but only a quiet calmness when they are around. You can be yourself and not worry about what they will think of you because they love you for who you are. The things that seem insignificant to most people such as a note, song or walk become invaluable treasures kept safe in your heart to cherish forever. Memories of your childhood come back and are so clear and vivid it's like being young again. Colors seem brighter and more brilliant. Laughter seems part of daily life where before it was infrequent or didn't exist at all. A phone call or two during the day helps to get you through a long day's work and always brings a smile to your face. In their presence, there's no need for continuous conversation, but you find you're quite content in just having them nearby.

Things that never interested you before become fascinating because you know they are important to this person who is so special to you. You think of this person on every occasion and in everything you do. Simple things bring them to mind like a pale blue sky, gentle wind or even a storm cloud on the horizon. You open your heart knowing that there's a chance it may be broken one day and in opening your heart, you experience a love and joy that you never dreamed possible. You find that being vulnerable is the only way to allow your heart to feel true pleasure that's so real it scares you. You find strength in knowing you have a true friend and possibly a soul mate who will remain loyal to the end. Life seems completely different, exciting and worthwhile. Your only hope and security is in knowing that they are a part of your life."

<u>Bob Marley</u>

BIOGRAPHY

Marianne LaValle-Vincent is a first-generation Italian-American. She has achieved numerous awards for her poetry and short stories throughout the United States and Europe. This is the author's 5th full length poetry collection. Other books include: *American Lie, 313's Child, Coverings and A Nice Italian Girl.*

Marianne has also written numerous short stories for the Chicken Soup for the Soul series, The Erma Bombeck Network, Humor at It's Best and Boomer Women Speak. Her poetry has infiltrated the internet on such sites as: Amarillo Bay, My Favorite Bullet, Poetic Diversity, Foliate Oak, Convergence and several internationally published anthologies.

When not hard at work managing an apartment complex, Marianne spends her free time with family. Still living in Syracuse, NY, she cooks every day and hosts Sunday dinners along with her sisters, Marge and Weez and her brother, John. Her three children: John, Albert and Jessica are always present as well as Grandchildren Brian, Joseph, Mariana and Alivia. Cousins, nieces, nephews and close friends are always invited. Marianne is happy to welcome you to her family feasts—just make sure to bring the vino!

"There is nothing more important than family. I am blessed to have my family members close by and we spend as much time as possible together. They provide comfort and a sense of belonging. It's what keeps me going."

Always interested in feedback, you can contact Marianne @ lavs4@hotmail.com.